S0-AZD-441

SIMPLY SENSATIONAL

Great Scarf Ideas

Great Scarf Ideas

CAROL ENDLER STERBENZ

Photography by Susan Bloch

CRESCENT BOOKS
NEW YORK ● AVENEL, NEW JERSEY

A FRIEDMAN GROUP BOOK

This 1994 edition published by Crescent Books, distributed by Outlet Book Company, Inc., a Random House Company,
40 Engelhard Avenue, Avenel, New Jersey 07001.

Random House
New York ● Toronto ● London ● Sydney ● Auckland

Text © 1993 by Carol Endler Sterbenz
Photography © 1993 Susan Bloch

All rights reserved. No part of this publication may be reproduced, stored in a retrieval system, or transmitted, in any form or by any means, electronic, photocopying, recording, or otherwise, without the prior written permission of the publisher.

ISBN 0-517-10301-X

SIMPLY SENSATIONAL:
GREAT SCARF IDEAS
was prepared and produced by
Michael Friedman Publishing Group, Inc.
15 West 26th Street
New York, New York 10010

Editor: Elizabeth Viscott Sullivan
Designer: Susan Livingston
Art Director: Jeff Batzli
Photography Editor: Christopher C. Bain
Illustrations: Kathy Bray

Color separations by Rainbow Graphic Arts Co., Ltd.
Printed and bound in China by Leefung-Asco Printers Ltd.

8 7 6 5 4 3 2 1

Every effort has been made to present the information in this book in a clear, complete, and accurate manner. It is important that all instructions be carefully followed, as failure to do so could result in injury. The publisher and the author expressly disclaim any and all liability resulting therefrom.

To Elizabeth Sullivan

Acknowledgments

I am grateful to the many friends and colleagues who generously supported this project: Elizabeth Sullivan, intuitive friend and talented editor, to whom this book is affectionately dedicated; Eileen and Michael Friedman, whose beautiful home provided the setting for each photograph, and whose congeniality and resourcefulness made a complex shooting schedule possible; Christopher Bain and Anne Price, for shepherding all elements of photography, as well as Susan Bloch, photographer, and Click model, Taxi; and Donita Williams, for her support and enthusiasm.

Many thanks to those who enthusiastically contributed the fine products shown here: Lynn Roberts of the Echo Design Group, Inc. for the scarves on pages 13, 15, 29, 37, 41, 45, 51, 55, 57, 65; Roy Chinicci, Gina Giordano, and Olga Llerena of V. Fraas for the scarves on pages 25, 27, 33, 39; Maureen Maguire and Sarah Patterson of Liz Claiborne, Inc. for the apparel on pages 19, 21, 63; Francine and Patricia Rexer of REXER-PARKES of Huntington, New York, for the apparel on pages 15, 17, 25, 27, 29, 39; Tara Gaffney of Capezio Ballet Makers for the ballet wear; and Debra Heller of Erwin PEARL, Inc. for the model's jewelry.

A special loving thanks to my children, Genevieve, Rodney, and Gabrielle, for being available to be draped and wrapped regardless of the hour, especially to Gabrielle, who contributed several of her own designs; and to my husband, John.

C.E.S.

CONTENTS

INTRODUCTION

It makes perfect sense that the scarf has enjoyed a long and imaginative history as a fashion accessory. After all, scarves are incredibly versatile. They are available in an astonishing array of fibers, textures, weaves, colors, and sizes. They can be arranged in a seemingly endless number of ways; draped, tied, folded, or wrapped, scarves help us to create personal statements of style. In an instant, a scarf can soften the formal line and cut of a dress, enhance a neckline, or add colorful drama to almost any ensemble. But a scarf can do more than add panache to an outfit; it can be transformed into apparel itself, from the Indian sari to the currently popular sarong, and even into accessory items and home furnishings.

The scarf has been an integral part of our wardrobes for more than three centuries. Although evidence places a long scarf squarely on the shoulders of the ecclesiastical dress of antiquity, the practice of draping fabric over the head, wrapping it around the neck, draping it around the shoulders, or allowing it to hang from neck to knee has not been confined to clerical groups alone. The scarf has enjoyed broad use while transforming itself in the process: in other words, the scarf has been appropriated by all social classes; it has crossed gender and geographical boundaries; and it has conferred class and celebrity to its wearers.

Of course, fashion is ever-changing, directly influencing the scarf's function as adornment and apparel; one can only anticipate that the scarf's use will continue to reflect current fashion trends. Nonetheless, looking beyond the world of fashion, it is quite clear that the scarf is consistently being used as a decorative accessory in the home. Whether used as a single item to add style and elegance to a table setting or combined with several others to create a soft home furnishing such as a duvet cover, the scarf is a useful decorative element in any living space, readily adaptable and fun to use.

This collection provides quick and easy projects that not only will help you to enhance your personal style, but also will inspire you to consider fresher, more innovative uses for the scarf. Here is a selection of classic wraps, drapes, and ties—all with an alluring twist. You'll also discover interesting ways to drape, tie, and arrange; creative but simple folding techniques; and a range of appealing accessory items and home furnishings, from a lingerie envelope to a lamp shade, window shade, and pillow sachet ensemble.

Finally, producing beautiful results with scarves is not only entertaining and gratifying, but requires only a minimal amount of time, very basic skills, and a few simple steps. The projects in this book will encourage you to try your hand at this rewarding art, to look beyond the traditional uses for the scarf, to personalize your wardrobe and home, and to invent new approaches to tying, draping, folding, and sewing as you go along.

PART I

HEAD, NECK,
and
SHOULDERS

Half Turban

Popular in the 1940s, the half turban takes on a contemporary look when made of a metallic stretch knit scarf tied in a classic topknot. The knit fabric allows the wrap to fit snugly and comfortably without slippage, while the metallic thread adds sparkle and elegance. Worn with or without a matching dickie and a sleek black jacket, this turban is the perfect way to dress up an outfit in an instant.

Stretch knits work best with this style, but silks and synthetics are good choices, too; with these fabrics, however, the topknot should be positioned closer to the forehead to minimize slippage and several bobby pins should be used to secure the scarf to the back of the head. Solid colors and overall designs are the most flattering patterns to use. Bold colors and textured fabrics will add the most visual interest.

Materials:

1 stretch knit scarf with metallic thread approximately 40 inches (100cm) long and 10 inches (25cm) wide

Directions:

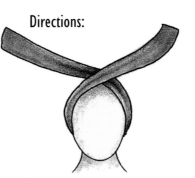

1. Holding ends of scarf firmly, place center of scarf at middle of back of neck, bringing remaining fabric to top of head.

2. Tie a knot at crown of head.

3. Tie a second knot.

4. Tuck ends of scarf
   under headbands
   formed by tying knots
   in steps 2 and 3.

5. Adjust knots and
   headbands by
   spreading fabric to
   create turban look.

Classic Headwrap

Nostalgic yet always modern, this particular headwrap has been associated with luminaries such as Greta Garbo, Marlene Dietrich, and Jacqueline Kennedy Onassis. A true classic, this versatile and simple style can change the mood of any outfit, as it looks terrific in virtually any weight fabric and/or pattern. It is important, though, to use a large square scarf that can be folded diagonally and whose ends are long enough to easily cross from underneath the chin to the back of the neck, where they are tied in a double knot.

You might want to try pairing a gauze scarf with a sheer blouse for a dressy look. For something more casual, coordinate a large polka-dot scarf with a crisp cotton blouse, a flared skirt, and cat's-eye sunglasses. To achieve both warmth and style in cooler weather, tie on a wool plaid scarf and tuck it into the collar of a short swing coat.

Materials:

1 scarf in animal print approximately 30 inches (75cm) square

Directions:

1. Lay scarf on a flat surface in the form of a diamond. Fold top point down 2 inches (1.25cm) past center point.

2. Place scarf over head and cross ends under chin.

3. Bring ends around to back of neck and tie in a double knot.

4. Tuck loose drape of scarf over knot to finish.

Headband

The appeal of this headband is its versatility: it can be made with any oblong scarf in any fabric, and it can be positioned on the head in various ways, from the crown to the nape of the neck. The streamers need not be tied in a bow; they can be permitted to cascade from underneath the hair and down the back, or they may be tucked underneath the bands to create a wider headband.

This headband can add interest to your wardrobe year-round. Here, a sheer white scarf with long streamers tied in a soft bow at the ear draws the eye to the scoop neck of a summer dress. Try pairing a leopard-print silk chiffon scarf with a blouse, suede shorts, and tights in autumn; a velvet scarf with a satin blouse and taffeta skirt in winter; or a paisley scarf with an oversized cotton V-neck sweater and a white, above-the-knee skirt in spring.

Materials:

1 oblong sheer scarf in white approximately 48 inches (120cm) long and 12 inches (30cm) wide

Directions:

1. Holding ends of scarf firmly, place center of scarf at middle of back of neck, bringing remaining fabric to top of head.

2. Tie a knot at crown of head.

3. Tie a bow.

4. Slide bow around head to just below right ear, allowing ends to cascade to shoulders.

Modified Ascot

The modified ascot is a very aristocratic look, particularly when tied in an elegant silk fabric that drapes easily about the neck. The modified ascot is also less formal than the traditional ascot, for the small front knots add a softer, more feminine touch. This ascot is extremely versatile and will complement far more than the standard blazer. Try pairing this scarf with a V-neck sweater or dress, or a suede, varsity-style jacket. The best scarf patterns for this look are smaller, overall designs, geometrics, and stripes.

Materials:

1 silk scarf approximately 30 inches (75cm) square

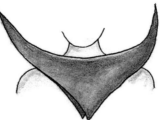

Directions:

1. Fold scarf in half diagonally to form a triangle.

2. Place center of scarf at front of neck.

3. Bring ends to back of neck and cross.

4. Bring ends to front again and tie two loose knots, spacing them evenly one above the other, and centering them below chin.

5. Arrange drape as desired.

Cravat and Tricolor Pocket Scarf

The look of a cravat tied in a perfect Windsor knot is sophisticated, and in this interpretation of the classic tie, men's tailoring becomes feminine and witty. A richly colored paisley scarf in emerald green, royal blue, and burgundy is worn with an oversized man's white shirt and a fitted navy blazer. Paired with an Annie Hall–style hat in camel, the whole ensemble alternates easily from formal to informal, despite the blue jeans. To create your own variation on this theme, consider matching a man's tuxedo jacket with a silk shirt and scarf, sewing on tiny beads to create a coordinated ensemble.

The fold used in the accompanying trio of pocket scarves is a popular variation of the Bishop's Hat, a fold often used for table napkins. Here, the three scarves are folded individually, then arranged to highlight the main colors of the cravat.

Materials for Cravat:

1 silk scarf in paisley pattern in emerald green, royal blue, and burgundy, approximately 30 inches (75cm) square

Directions:

Folded Band:

1. Lay scarf on a flat surface in the form of a diamond.

2. Fold top point down 2 inches (5cm) past center point.

3. Fold bottom point up 2 inches past center point so that it overlaps upper section.

4. Fold upper section along long edge to center point.

5. Fold bottom section along long edge to center point.

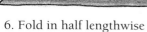

6. Fold in half lengthwise to form folded band.

7. To make cravat, tie folded band as described in directions on page 22.

Cravat:

1. Center folded band at back of neck; bring ends to front.

2. Pull right end down so that it is two-thirds longer than left end.

3. Cross longer end in front of shorter end; wrap longer end behind shorter end and bring it around to front. Lift longer end up toward neck, then over and behind short end.

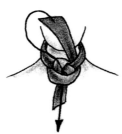

4. Wrap longer end around front of shorter end; bring long end behind short end.

5. Lift longer end up toward chin and down through loop now formed at front.

6. Adjust cravat by sliding knot along shorter end.

Materials for Tricolor Pocket Scarf:

3 pocket scarves (emerald green, royal blue, and burgundy), each approximately 12 inches (30cm) square

Directions:

1. Fold one pocket scarf in half diagonally to form a triangle. Center point should face upward.

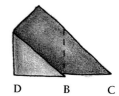

2. Fold left bottom point (A) one-third of the way across scarf to point (B).

3. Fold right bottom point (C) back to point (D).

5. Repeat steps 1–4 with the two remaining scarves.

4. Hold folds in place and turn scarf over.

6. Lay one folded scarf on top of the other so that each scarf overlaps the one adjacent to it.

7. Hold scarves together and insert into breast pocket of jacket, making sure that a diagonal slip of each color shows above the top edge of the pocket.

Neck Drape

Effortless to tie and always flattering, this scarf design adds sophistication while it softens the neckline of any dress or shirt by introducing a curve and a splash of color. A brooch or decorative pin can be used to secure the scarf at the collar and to add interesting detail. To vary the look of this simple drape, arrange the scarf so that it lies smoothly under a shirt or dress collar, then tie it in a loose knot just below the collar opening.

This scarf design works nicely with any oblong scarf; the length of the scarf simply determines the overall effect. For a modified ascot, knot a very short scarf at the center of the neck, spread the drape across the knot, and tuck the ends into the open neck of a starched white shirt. In cooler weather, tie a very long, fringed wool scarf under the collar of a belted coat, bringing the ends to one side and slipping them underneath the belt so that they overlap slightly at the bottom; this will create a neat, layered effect.

Materials:

1 oblong silk scarf in floral pattern approximately 48 inches (120cm) long and 10 inches (25cm) wide

Decorative pin or brooch

Directions:

1. Loop scarf around neck and cross ends at left shoulder.

2. Make a loose knot. Secure knot with brooch or decorative pin and allow ends of scarf to drape softly to front and back of shoulder.

Shoulder Drape

The understated elegance of this drape belies the simplicity of its arrangement. Placed off-center and tied on the shoulder, the scarf's sensuous folds soften the straight lines of a dress and add a charming contrast.

Small Velcro dots are an easy way to keep this wrap firmly in place; just strategically position the dots on the underside of the scarf and on top of the garment, and press them together. Using Velcro dots also enables you to use smoother, lighter fabrics, such as rayon, silk, and satin, as these tend to slide about if they are not held down in some way.

Materials:

1 silk scarf in floral pattern approximately 30 inches (75cm) square

Small Velcro dots

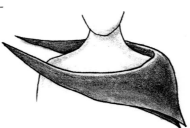 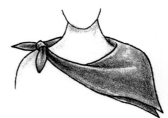

Directions:

1. Fold scarf in half diagonally to form a triangle.

2. Place scarf on shoulders, centering bottom point on left shoulder.

3. Tie ends into a loose double knot on right shoulder.

4. Arrange folds of scarf; use Velcro dots to firmly position drape, if necessary.

Shoulder Wrap

This pretty wrap made from a floral scarf highlights the neckline and enfolds the shoulders, and is also beautiful when worn with a strapless dress. When fringe, tassels, or beadwork is added to the selvages, the wrap is an ideal complement to evening wear. For a less formal look, try pairing a white cotton strapless top with a shoulder wrap in a compatible cotton. The best scarves for this style are those that tend to stay in place, so choose fabrics that are rougher rather than smoother in texture. This design can be easily adapted for any season simply by using scarves of different weights and colors.

Materials:

1 scarf in floral pattern approximately 40 inches (100cm) square

Directions:

1. Fold scarf in half diagonally to form a triangle.

2. Centering scarf on back, bring ends forward and place scarf just off the shoulders.

3. Tie ends into a double knot at center of chest.

4. Adjust folds of scarf as necessary.

PART 2

APPAREL

Sarong and Neck Drape

Although usually thought of as summer or resort wear, the sarong is a wonderful style for the cooler months when made of a heavier-weave fabric and paired with tights and a short jacket. The sarong shown here is reversible, for the jacquard scarf of which it is made naturally emphasizes a different color on either side of the fabric. The additional beauty of this sarong is that the flattering drape of the fabric creates sensual folds that lead the eye from hip to hip; the addition of a small chain-link belt further accentuates the effect. For summer, try making the sarong of cotton or rayon scarves that have interesting weaves. You can also pair the sarong with a unitard or simple T-shirt, and wear it higher on the waist for a different look.

The accompanying neck scarf is draped simply around the throat so that the ends fall to the back and dangle freely. The scarf is not tied at all. A cashmerelike fiber is a good choice, for it is soft yet weighty enough not to slip off the shoulders.

Materials for Sarong:

1 fringed jacquard scarf in navy and magenta approximately 48 inches (120cm) square

 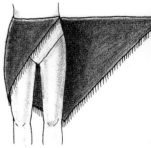

Directions:

1. Lay scarf on a flat surface in the form of a diamond.

2. Fold top point down to center point of scarf to form fold for waistband.

3. Place top fold of scarf at back of waist, sliding scarf off-center by pulling left end forward slightly.

4. Bring right end of scarf across front of waist; hold in place.

5. Bring left end of scarf around and across front of waist so that it overlaps short end of scarf.

6. Finish by tucking left end into top of waistband, adjusting leftover fabric as necessary.

Materials for Neck Drape:

1 oblong wool scarf in magenta approximately 60 inches (150cm) long and 15 inches (37.5cm) wide

Directions:

1. Place center of scarf across front of neck.

2. Bring ends over shoulders, allowing them to hang down loosely at the back.

3. Adjust front of scarf to full width, if desired.

Kilt and Shoulder Shawl

This kilt and shoulder shawl design takes advantage of the natural luxury and comfort of cashmere. The simple wrapped skirt, encircled by a chain belt and complemented by a stretch bodysuit and a pair of tights, is easy elegance at its best.

This pattern is best suited to heavier-weight scarves and is readily adaptable to a variety of fabrics. The length of the kilt is dictated by the width of the scarf you use, although this can be altered easily; by adjusting the width of the flap of fabric that forms the waistband, you can lengthen or shorten the skirt to suit your taste.

The shoulder shawl is stylishly bulky. A casual wrap, it has a romantic, stolelike look.

Materials for Kilt:

1 fringed scarf in black-and-white checkerboard pattern approximately 80 inches (200cm) long and 40 inches (100cm) wide

Chain-link belt in gold

Directions:

1. Lay scarf horizontally on a flat surface.

2. Fold over a 3-inch- (7.5cm) wide strip from top of long edge; flatten fold with fingers. (Remember, you can adjust the fold to make the kilt longer or shorter.)

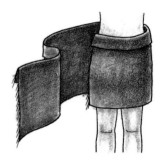

3. To wrap kilt, begin at back of left hip. Pull scarf across back to right hip, then across front to left hip.

4. Repeat step 3, ending at front of left hip.

5. Tuck gathered section of scarf into waistband, allowing remaining length to cascade along front to the side.

6. Adjust as necessary. Finish with gold chain-link belt.

Materials for Shoulder Shawl:

1 fringed wool scarf in red approximately 72 inches (180cm) long and 18 inches (45cm) wide

Directions:

1. Center scarf on back and wrap around shoulders.

2. Cross ends at front of chest and tie in a loose knot.

3. Tuck ends under shawl at shoulders. Adjust drape and folds as desired.

Strapless Top

Simple but elegant, this strapless top can be made using a wool scarf (as shown) or a heavier-weight silk fabric. The appeal of this wrap is that you can combine a traditional plaid wool or taffeta scarf with a velvet skirt, or black silk trousers or shorts, to achieve a formal yet innovative holiday look. The contours of the front of the top contrast with the lines of the bustle in back and introduce an element of interest. Should you wish to omit the bustle, allow the ends of the scarf to dangle in two layers below the back of the waist.

Materials:

1 wool scarf in red and green plaid approximately 68 inches (170cm) long and 24 inches (60cm) wide

Kilt pin

Directions:

1. Lay scarf horizontally on a flat surface.
2. Fold over a 3-inch-(7.5cm) wide strip of long edge of scarf, flattening fold with fingers.

Remember to secure the first knot (see step 4) with a kilt pin in order to prevent the top from slipping down. Be careful when inserting the pointed end of the pin into the scarf so that you avoid splitting the fibers of the scarf—and sticking yourself.

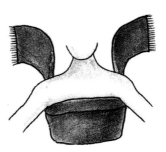

3. Place scarf at center front of chest, folded edge facing outward.

4. Bring ends to back and tie a knot; secure knot with kilt pin.

5. Tuck loose top end of
   scarf under knot to
   form a bustlelike loop.
   Adjust folds evenly.

6. Tuck loose bottom end
   of scarf under knot to
   form a second loop.

7. Make sure bottom loop
   shows beneath top
   loop. Adjust folds of
   bottom loop to resem-
   ble those of top loop.

Skirt and Bandeau

When made using pastel scarves, this summer skirt and bandeau is a youthful look, but one that readily becomes more sophisticated when created with silk scarves in classic colors such as burgundy, navy, and white. For this pattern, two layers of sheer silk scarves are gathered into an above-the-knee skirt; a coordinating scarf, folded diagonally then twisted slightly, forms a cummerbundlike waistband. The skirt looks charming with the bandeau, but it also looks well with a bodysuit, bathing suit, or close-fitting T-shirt.

This design can easily be made formal. Try fashioning the skirt from scarves in black tulle and wearing it with a velvet strapless top and tulle shawl.

The bandeau is made by simply folding a scarf and twisting it once at its center; whether tied or fastened with hooks and eyes at the back, this top can be worn under a sheer blouse or paired with shorts or jeans.

Materials for Skirt:

5 pastel sheer scarves, each approximately 36 inches (90cm) square

Thread to match

Directions:

1. Lay four scarves on a flat surface so that adjacent selvages touch.

2. Sew scarves together at adjacent selvages to form one long strip.

3. Fold strip in half from top to bottom. Pin fold to secure; fold will form waistband.

4. Approximately ½ inch (1.25cm) below fold, baste a row of loose running stitches across entire scarf. (Basting will form waistband.)

5. Repeat step 4 to create a second row that is ¼ inch (6mm) below the first row.

6. Gently pull basting to form gathers across waistband and to achieve desired waist measurement; top-stitch into place.

7. Fold remaining scarf into cummerbund as shown above. Stitch along top and bottom to secure.

8. Center and pin cummerbund to front of waistband, right sides facing, edges even; leave scarf ends free for tying in back.

9. Stitch waistband into place.

Materials for Bandeau:

1 pastel sheer scarf approximately 36 inches (90cm) square

Thread to match

3 sets of hooks and eyes

Directions:

1. Lay scarf on a flat surface; fold in half from top to bottom.

2. Fold in half again from top to bottom to form bandeau.

3. Sew layers together at each short end of bandeau to secure.

4. Form three narrow gathers at each short end of bandeau; sew gathers in place.

5. Fasten hooks to one short edge of the bandeau, eyes to the other.

6. Lay bandeau on a flat surface and twist fabric once at center.

Kimono

Despite the stark lines intrinsic to traditional kimono design, this version of the kimono has a soft, romantic look by virtue of the lush pattern of the scarves from which it was made. Very easy to construct and adaptable to most large, square scarves of any fabric, this kimono is made from only three scarves and requires a bare minimum of sewing experience.

When choosing scarves for your kimono, consider fiber and weight first. Cotton scarves are lightweight and can breathe, so they are suitable for wear during the warmer months. Wools and wool blends are also comfortable and provide warmth during the cooler months. Thereafter, the choice of color and design is a question of personal taste. Overall patterns of bold geometrics and stripes work well, although paisleys, stripes, and small prints will create a less sophisticated but no less charming effect.

Materials:

3 scarves in floral pattern, each approximately 40 inches (100cm) square

Thread to match

Silk cord for belt (optional)

The full width of a 40-inch (100cm) square scarf may make the kimono larger than desired. To make a smaller kimono, cut an equal amount off the side selvages of each of two of the scarves used for the body of the robe. You can use the trim to create a simple sash to tie the kimono.

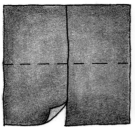

Directions:

1. Cut two of the scarves in half. One set of halves will become the sleeves; the other will become the front panels of the kimono.

2. Lay the third scarf, right side up, on a flat surface. This is the back of the kimono.

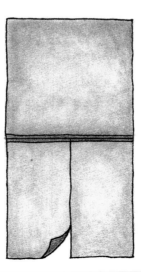

3. To make up kimono front, place one set of half-panels, right side down, on top of the kimono back. Selvages should be at center front.

4. Stitch half-panels to top edge of kimono back to create "shoulders." Iron shoulder seams flat.

5. With right side of pattern facing up, lay entire construction flat.

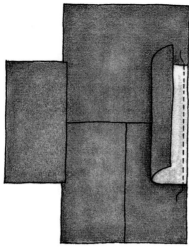

8. To finish, fold entire construction in half across shoulder line, lining up front and back pieces. (Make sure sleeves are of even width.) Beginning at bottom of each sleeve, sew in toward kimono body, then down to hem to complete robe.

9. To make belt, cut silk cord to waist size plus 18 inches (45cm). Center cord at back of kimono, tack to fabric, and bring ends to front for tying.

6. To construct first sleeve, mark one half-panel from second set at top and bottom center edges with pins. Lay panel against kimono body so that shoulder seam and pin at top center edge of sleeve are aligned. Sleeve should be right side up, edges even. Pin and sew pieces together.

7. Repeat step 6 with second half-panel to create second sleeve.

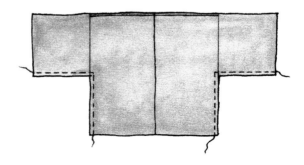

ACCESSORIES
and
HOME FURNISHINGS

Clutch Purse

Generally carried for its aesthetic appeal rather than for its function, a unique clutch purse can add real style to any outfit. The design of this small evening purse is classic, particularly as it is made from a bold yet elegant striped scarf. A sparkling brooch in faux marcasite decorates the top flap, enhancing the overall charm.

Since this design is well suited for scarves of any fabric, it is compatible with both formal and casual clothing. A black linen clutch made to coordinate with a black linen sheath is understated but timeless and chic. Made from more unusual fabric, the clutch can add pizzazz and wit to a suit, a shirtdress, or the popular trio of blue jeans, T-shirt, and blazer.

Materials:

1 oblong silk scarf in blue and white stripes approximately 32 inches (80cm) long and 10 inches (25cm) wide

Polyester batting approximately 16 inches long (40cm) and 10 inches (25cm) wide

Thread to match

Decorative pin or brooch

Directions:

1. Lay scarf vertically on a flat surface; fold in half from top to bottom. One side will act as lining of finished purse.

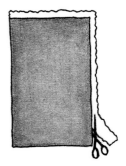

2. Place folded scarf on batting. Trim batting to size of folded scarf.

3. Pin batting to "lining" side of folded scarf; make sure all layers are flat and that there are no buckles.

4. Baste all layers into place. Remove pins.

5. Mark and cut two sections of the purse as shown at right; the proportions should be approximately one-third (for the pouch) and two-thirds (for the fold) of total scarf length. Trim corners of each section into the curved shapes shown.

6. Sew a ¼-inch (6mm) seam around outside edges of each section; leave an opening for turning batting inside finished purse.

7. Trim corners, clip curves, and turn fabric right side out; slip-stitch opening shut.

8. Using a cool iron and/or press cloth, iron seams flat.

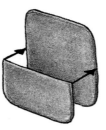

9. To form purse, place smaller section onto bottom half of larger section. Pin and slip-stitch along sides and bottom of smaller section to create pouch.

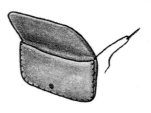

10. Place brooch or decorative pin on top section as shown.

Lingerie Envelope

There is something wonderfully indulgent about tucking away lingerie in a special envelope all its own, especially in this one made from a lush silk-fringed, rose-covered scarf. This lingerie envelope closes with a simple loop-over-button clasp and is as easy to make as it is elegant.

This design is quite versatile. For a less formal look, use a cotton scarf. You can even convert the envelope into a shoulder bag by sewing on a shoulder strap made of cord. To make a bigger envelope, use a larger oblong scarf with the same proportions given in the directions. However, you can also change the proportions by folding the scarf in fourths, thus creating one pocket on each side of the center fold. The lingerie envelope makes a lovely gift.

Materials:

1 double-layered, fringed silk scarf approximately 60 inches (150cm) long and 15 inches (37.5cm) wide

Thread to match

Frog, or decorative cord and button

Directions:

1. Lay scarf vertically on a flat surface, wrong side up.

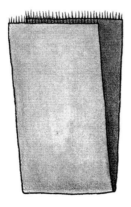

2. Fold scarf in half so that wrong sides face each other.

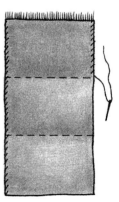

3. Sew long sides of scarf closed; tack short, fringed side closed.

4. To form pouch, fold bottom third of scarf upward so that it fully covers center portion of scarf. Using a blind or hem stitch, sew two sides of fold closed (top of fold will form pouch opening).

5. To form finished envelope, fold top third of scarf onto pouch. Sew decorative loop to bottom center of top flap.

6. Sew decorative button to center of pocket where loop overlaps.

Tablecloth and Seat Covers

A tablecloth makes it possible to transform a table from mundane to remarkable. The effect is immediate: the mood of a dining area can change in the time it takes to slip one cloth off a table and lay on another. Add china, glassware, and silverware to the mix, and the decorating options become virtually infinite.

Scarves are an exciting resource for enhancing the table. They can be used alone, such as the black-and-white striped scarf emblazoned with sunflowers shown here, or they can be sewn together to create a decorating statement that is appealing in its own right. Compatible patterns range from country prints to retro designs from the 1950s, when fruit and floral designs were popular. Elegant tapestry and embroidery designs are easy to find, as are thematic patterns, such as sailing and riding. It's easy to combine prints, solids, florals, and paisleys—just use one or two colors as an organizing principle.

To further coordinate a table area, you can also use scarves to cover seat cushions. Simply remove the cushion from the frame of the chair, tack the scarf in place, then return the cushion to the frame. For a less permanent effect, lay an oversized scarf over the seat cushion and tie the ends to the back of the chair.

Cottons and cotton blends are the most practical choices for tablecloths and seat covers—they are durable and washable. Rayon, linen, and silk are lovely, but they require extra care.

Materials for Tablecloth and Setting:

1 scarf in striped and floral pattern approximately 40 inches (100cm) square

Tablecloth in coordinating background color

Coordinating napkins

Directions:

1. Lay background cloth over table; smooth buckles as necessary.

Materials for Seat Cover:

1 scarf in coordinating print

Directions:

1. Center coordinating scarf over seat cushion; smooth buckles as necessary.
2. Tuck edges between cushion and chair. Fasten with upholstery tacks to secure or tie back ends to back of chair frame.

2. Lay scarf over tablecloth so that it is centered; allow corners to fall over table edge.

3. Set table as desired, using coordinating napkins.

Window Shade, Lamp Shade, and Sachet Pillows

The scarf is an easy way to enhance the decor of a living space, whether you use it to add a dash of color or integrate it into an overall theme. The appeal of this approach to decorating is that you can alter the look of a room without investing a lot of money or time. Best of all, the results are immediate and beautiful.

In this particular case, a narrow window shelf in a guest bathroom needed to be spruced up. The window shades were made from oblong scarves sewn along their selvages and strung across a silk cord; the lamp shade cover is a simple sleeve made from a scarf that was gathered and placed over the existing shade; and the coordinating sachets are miniature pillows filled with polyester and fragrant potpourri.

Materials for Window Shade:

2 oblong silk scarves, each approximately 48 inches (120cm) long and 10 inches (25cm) wide

Thread to match

12 small curtain rings

Coordinating silk cord cut to width of window

2 thumbtacks

To assure that your window shade is large enough to fully cover the window frame, measure the width of the frame before you begin; doing so will help you determine both the number of scarves you will need and the individual measurement of each scarf. The window shade is gently gathered, so allow extra width for each panel. In general, the panel should be 1½ times wider than the window.

Directions:

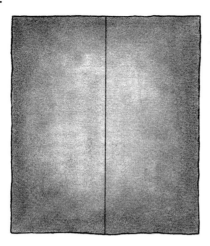

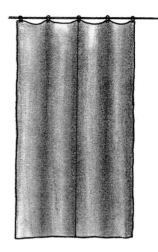

1. Cut each oblong scarf in half widthwise; hem raw edges.

2. To form one window panel, pin and stitch two scarf sections together at long side of selvages; right sides should face each other.

3. Repeat step 2 to create a second panel.

4. Stitch small curtain rings at even intervals across length of top selvage.

5. Thread silk cord through rings and suspend window shade across window frame. Tack ends of shade into place with thumbtacks.

This shade is intended primarily for decorative purposes. Therefore, it is best to put the scarf covering on a lamp that is not in constant use and takes a low-watt light bulb. Be certain that the shade and scarf are at a safe distance from the light bulb to avoid fire.

Materials for Lamp Shade:

1 oblong scarf approximately 2 inches (5cm) wider and 1½ times the circumference of any ready-made lamp shade

Thread to match

½-inch- (1.25cm) wide ribbon

Narrow elastic

Directions:

1. On wrong side of scarf, pin a strip of ribbon so that it runs full-length and even with top selvage. Sew top and bottom ribbon selvages to scarf to form casing for elastic.

2. Repeat step 1 to form casing at bottom selvage of scarf.

3. Cut two lengths of elastic, each 2 inches (5cm) longer than casing. Thread elastic through casing at top and bottom; knot ends to temporarily secure them.

4. Place scarf over lamp shade, pulling elastic at top and bottom until gathers form evenly around the shade. When fabric is adjusted snugly around shade, sew elastic ends to secure.

Materials for Sachet Pillows:

2 pocket scarves (each scarf makes 2 pillows) in coordinating colors, each approximately 12 inches (30cm) square

Thread and $\frac{1}{16}$-inch- (1.6mm) wide satin ribbon to match

Polyester stuffing

Potpourri

Directions:

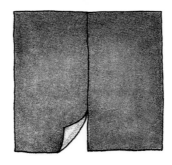

1. Cut one pocket scarf in half.

2. Fold in half widthwise. Right side should face inward, and edges should be even.

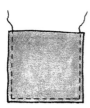

3. Pin and stitch around three sides, leaving one side with selvage open for turning; clip corners and turn to right side. Iron flat.

4. Loosely fill case with polyester stuffing; add potpourri to well in center of stuffing.

5. Slip-stitch opening to close.

6. Repeat steps 1–5 to create additional sachet pillows.

7. Arrange pillows in a bundle; tie them with satin ribbon.

Duvet Cover and Pillowcases

There is no greater comfort than that of a four-poster bed adorned with plump pillows and cozy quilts made from cottons in soothing colors. This bedroom conveys such warmth; large cotton scarves displaying medallions of peaches and roses set against a field of blue-and-white gingham check were sewn together to make an oversized patchwork duvet cover and matching European-style pillows. The bold bands of royal blue provide a cue for other decorative accessories, such as a ceramic pitcher of wildflowers or a collection of blue ceramic dishes.

For a more formal look, you might use scarves in silk, satin, wool, or brocade. For an Amish-inspired duvet cover, try using solid silk pocket squares in gold, turquoise, purple, black, magenta, and rose. When you approach scarves as an element for patchwork, vast possibilities open up.

The pleasure of this project extends beyond its romantic, serene look, for the duvet cover and pillowcases can be made in an afternoon.

Materials for Duvet Cover:

6 cotton scarves in floral print, each approximately 30 inches (75cm) square

Thread to match

White cotton fabric or bedsheet, 62 inches (155cm) wide and 92 inches (230cm) long

18 inches (45cm) grosgrain ribbon

Heavier-weave scarves, preferably cotton, are the best choice for this project.

Directions:

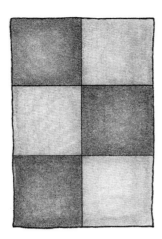

Front of Duvet Cover:

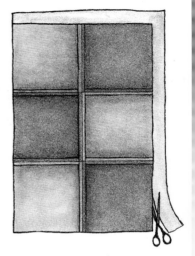

Back of Duvet Cover:

1. Lay scarves on a flat surface in a six-block pattern as shown above.

2. Sew top two scarves together at center, right sides facing, selvages even; iron seam flat.

3. Repeat step 2 with middle and bottom pairs of scarves.

4. Sew all three pairs together across center selvages to complete six-block pattern.

1. Lay white cotton fabric right side up on a flat surface.

2. Position front of duvet cover over fabric so that right sides face each other.

3. Trim cotton fabric to size of front of duvet.

Assembly:

1. To form duvet case, sew two side and bottom edges closed. Clip corners and turn to right side.

2. To form tie that secures duvet within case, cut ribbon in half. Sew one half to inside center point of top front and other to inside center point of top back of case.

3. Slip duvet into case; tie ribbon.

Materials for Pillowcases:

2 cotton scarves in same floral print as duvet cover, each approximately 30 inches (75cm) square

Thread to match

White cotton fabric or bedsheet, 72 inches (180cm) wide and 60 inches (150cm) long

2 ready-made square pillows, slightly smaller than finished size of pillowcase

Directions:

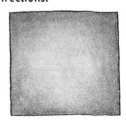

Front of Pillow:

The front of each pillow is made up of one scarf.

Back of Pillow:

1. Lay white cotton fabric on a flat surface, right side up.

2. Measure and cut two sections, each 30 inches (75cm) long and 18 inches (45cm) wide.

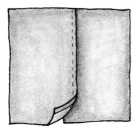

3. Sew a ½-inch (1.25cm) hem on one long edge of each section, as shown above.

4. With right sides facing up, overlap back sections so that their combined width is 30 inches (75cm); pin and sew sections together.

Assembly:

1. Lay scarf (front of pillow) on a flat surface, right side up.

2. Position pillow backing over front with right sides facing.

3. Sew four sides together to form pillowcase. (If your pillow form is smaller than the dimensions of the finished case made here, sew a seam along all four sides of the case, making sure the distance is even all around. This will the overall measurement of the case.)

4. Clip corners and turn right side out.

5. Slip pillow into case through opening at back.

APPENDICES

OTHER SCARF IDEAS

*T*o recycle a worn scarf, dye it a compatible color or use the intact portions to create small accessories, such as the sachet pillows or any of the other smaller projects mentioned in this book. ❧ To decorate the hearth of a fireplace in summer, shirr several oblong scarves, in coordinating or identical colors and patterns, across expandable café rods and place them within the opening of the hearth. ❧ To make a poncho, cut a keyhole-shaped opening in the center of a large scarf; bind off the raw edges with a blind or hem stitch. ❧ To decorate a hat with a wide brim, simply tie a scarf around the crown, allowing the ends to dangle over the brim. ❧ To show off a special scarf, simply place it in a picture frame and hang it. ❧ To make your own scarves, sew together any combination of cottons, silks, or synthetics that you find appealing. You can decorate the scarves with sequins, beads, fringe, or anything else that suits your fancy. ❧ To coordinate two scarves, add fringe, beads, or lace to the selvages of each.

SCARF CARE

FIBER	DRY-CLEAN	WASH				DRYING TEMPERATURE	IRON SETTING	NOTES
		HAND	MACHINE	WATER TEMPERATURE	MILD DETERGENT			
Cotton	Yes	Yes	Yes	Hot	Yes	Medium	High (Iron when damp.)	Fabric softener recommended. Do not overdry.
Linen	Yes*	Yes	Yes	Warm	Yes	Low	High (Iron when very damp.)	Wash if label says "pre-shrunk."
Silk	Yes*	Yes	No	Lukewarm	Yes	Low	Low (Iron on wrong side.)	Wash if label says "washable." Avoid prolonged exposure to sunlight.
Wool	Yes*	Yes	No	Cool	No	—	Medium (Iron with damp press cloth.)	Do not machine-dry.
Synthetics	Yes	Yes	Yes	Lukewarm	Yes	Medium	Low–Medium	Follow cleaning instructions on label.

*Preferred cleaning method

INDEX